Mindful Magic

DREAMY BEDTIME MEDITATIONS
for Children

Embark of Sleepytime Adventures to Calm,
Soothe Nighttime Anxiety,
& Drift into Peaceful Slumber

Kaela Green Carter M.S., CSP

*To my children;
Gemma, Lila, & Christian...
& all the world's children...
Illuminate the light within
to guide us into a brighter tomorrow.*

Contents

Introduction

Why Bedtime Meditations?   1

Chapter 1

The Power of Bedtime Meditations   4

The Importance of Quality Sleep for Children's Development   4

The Magic of Mindfulness and Meditation   7

Benefits of Meditation on Mental and Emotional Health   9

Exploring the Science Behind Meditation and Sleep   12

Chapter 2

Getting Started with Bedtime Meditations   15

Creating a Soothing Atmosphere in the Bedroom   15

Creating a Calm and Relaxing Bedtime Routine   18

Addressing Bedtime Worries and Anxiety 20

Chapter 3
Mindfulness Techniques for Children 22

Mindfulness Practices 23

Mindful Breathing Techniques 25

Visualizations and Guided Imagery 27

Chapter 4
Engaging Parent-Child Bonding through Bedtime Meditations 30

The Role of Affection and Connection in Meditation Practices 30

Fostering Positive Communication and Mindful Listening 33

Chapter 5
Empowering Children with Self-Meditation Techniques 35

Teaching Children Self-Meditation Skills 35

Encouraging Children to Express Their Emotions 38

Chapter 6

Fun Activities to Support Bedtime Meditations   **40**

Crafting Dreamcatchers for Sweet Dreams   41

Creating Dream Journals to Capture Magical Moments   44

Playing Relaxing Music for Peaceful Sleep   46

Dreamy Bedtime Meditations for Children   **48**

Chapter 7

Maintaining Consistency and Forming Lasting Habits   **49**

The Importance of Consistency   49

Chapter 8

Guided Bedtime Meditations   **54**

Guided Meditation: Cloud Dreaming   55

Guided Meditation: Starlight Voyage   60

Guided Meditation: The Enchanted Forest   65

Guided Meditation: Deep Sea Adventure   69

Guided Meditation: The Magical Garden   73

Guided Meditation: Island of Dreams	77
Guided Meditation: The Lullaby Express	81
Guided Meditation: Unicorn Dreamland	86

Conclusion

Embracing the Magic	**90**
About the Author	94
The Mindful Magic Series	**95**
Bibliography	97
Connect with Kaela Green Carter	**99**

Mindful Magic

Dreamy Bedtime Meditations for Children

Why Bedtime Meditations?

In today's fast-paced, over-stimulating world, it can be extremely challenging for children to wind down before bedtime. The busy hustle of daily life, coupled with the constant exposure to screens and technology, can make it difficult for children to relax at the end of the day. Sound familiar?

As parents, we know this all too well and have likely experienced nights we wished we could wave a magic wand that would instantly drift our children off to dreamland. We all can certainly use a bit of magic in our bedtime routines and this is where meditation comes into play, offering an invaluable solution for parents seeking to enhance their child's sleep routine.

Bedtime meditations are a powerful tool that can help children transition from the mad rush of the day to a state of deep relaxation. Guided meditations provide a structured and soothing experience, which allows children to let go of any anxiety or stress they might be feeling.

These meditations are specifically designed to help children cultivate a sense of calmness and peace, while also promoting positive thoughts and emotions. One of the key benefits of sleep meditations is that they can effectively alleviate nighttime worries and anxiety in children.

Sleep meditations create a safe space for children to confront and release the fears, worries, and insecurities that often prevent them from falling asleep. By practicing these meditations regularly, children can develop healthy coping mechanisms and a sense of emotional resilience.

Moreover, bedtime meditations significantly improve the quality of sleep our children are getting. As they embark on a guided journey through their imagination, children naturally enter a state of deep relaxation, making it easier for them to fall asleep and stay asleep throughout the night.

Meditations before sleep also help children establish a consistent sleep routine, enhancing their overall sleep quality. For parents, incorporating bedtime meditations into their child's nightly routine has numerous advantages.

Not only does it allow parents to spend quality time with their children before bed, but it also creates a peaceful atmosphere that fosters connection and tranquility. By engaging in these meditations together, parents and children can bond, share experiences, and create lasting memories.

Bedtime meditations offer a host of benefits for children. From promoting relaxation and better sleep quality to relieving anxiety and fostering emotional well-being, the meditations in this book provide a valuable tool for parents, along with scientifically proven strategies and techniques that can serve as a handy guide for better bedtimes.

By understanding the importance of bedtime meditations and implementing them into their child's nightly routine, parents can help their children find peace and tranquility, promoting a restful night's sleep and a positive mindset.

Chapter
1

The Power of Bedtime Meditations

The Importance of Quality Sleep for Children's Development

As parents, we all want the best for our children. Of course, we want them to be healthy, happy, and successful in all aspects of life, however, we often underestimate the importance of quality sleep in their development. In fact, quality sleep plays a very significant role in children's development and, believe it or not, is one of the most crucial factors impacting their overall well-being.

Let's explore the importance of quality sleep for children's development and how it can positively impact their lives. Sleep is not only vital for physical growth but also for cognitive and emotional development.

During sleep, the brain consolidates and processes the information it has gathered throughout the day. This process is essential for memory formation and learning. Adequate sleep ensures that your child's brain is ready to absorb new knowledge, as well as to effectively retain it.

Furthermore, proper sleep plays a critical role in regulating emotions. You may notice that when children don't get enough sleep, they tend to become irritable, moody, and have difficulty managing their feelings. Oftentimes, sleep deprivation can also lead to behavioral problems, including attention issues and hyperactivity.

Who would have thought that by simply ensuring our children get enough sleep, we can actually help them develop emotional resilience and better prepare them to cope with life's daily challenges? Sleep is also essential for physical growth and development. While a child sleeps, the body releases growth hormones that promote the development of muscles, bones, and other tissues.

Adequate sleep is especially crucial during the early years when children experience rapid growth. One of the most impactful ways you can contribute to your child's overall physical health and well-being is to ensure they get enough sleep. Have you ever wondered what we, as parents can do to make sure our children are getting the quality sleep their bodies and brains require for optimal functioning?

Establishing a consistent bedtime routine is key. By creating a predictable routine, which children can perform and count on nightly we set the stage for them to begin to take bedtime into their own hands. Incorporating relaxation techniques, such as mindfulness and bedtime meditations, can help create a calm and peaceful environment that promotes sleep.

The independence children will be able to develop through a regular nightly practice of their routine will help to eliminate bedtime battles, while helping them to wind down more easily and achieve a more peaceful slumber.

In conclusion, quality sleep is essential for children's development, as it impacts their cognitive, emotional, and physical well-being. By prioritizing sleep and establishing a bedtime routine that includes relaxation techniques like bedtime meditations, parents can support their children's overall growth and development. So, tuck your little ones into bed and let the magic of meditation and quality sleep pave the way for their bright future.

The Magic of Mindfulness and Meditation

The topics of 'mindfulness and meditation' have been trending for some time now. In fact, these concepts seem to grow increasingly more and more popular as the importance of mental health is called into our collective awareness. But what is all the hype about? In what ways are mindfulness and meditation beneficial for our children?

Research has shown that practicing mindfulness and meditation can have a profound impact on a child's well-being and overall development. By introducing these practices at an early age, we are equipping our children with essential tools to navigate the challenges of life, promote emotional regulation, and cultivate a sense of inner peace.

Isn't that what we all want for our children? So why aren't these concepts being taught in schools? Well, it does boggle the mind—believe me, I know. But that, I'm afraid is a topic for another book, so for now, let us continue to delve into mindfulness.

Mindfulness encourages children to be fully present in the moment, fostering self-awareness and the ability to focus their attention. Through guided meditations, they learn to observe their thoughts and emotions without judgment, allowing them to better understand and manage their feelings.

This skill becomes invaluable as they grow, helping them cope with stress, anxiety, and other emotional struggles. Meditation also supports the development of a calm and relaxed state, helping to prepare children to fall asleep more easily, and to remain in a peaceful slumber throughout the night.

Knowing how crucial a good night's sleep is for our little ones' physical and mental well-being, we can understand just how beneficial mindfulness can be. By teaching mindfulness techniques to our children, we not only build their awareness of their thoughts and feelings in the present moment but also provide them with a valuable tool that will help them learn to better regulate their emotions and handle whatever trials life throws their way.

By incorporating bedtime meditations into your child's nightly bedtime routine, you are able to create a serene atmosphere for them to release any worries or fears, promoting deep and restorative sleep.

Benefits of Meditation on Mental and Emotional Health

It's no secret that, nowadays, children are constantly bombarded with stimuli from a young age, leading to increased stress and anxiety. As parents, it is crucial for us to help our children develop healthy coping mechanisms to navigate through life's challenges. One effective tool that has gained popularity in recent years, although it has existed for centuries, is meditation.

Utilizing meditations for kids at bedtime offers numerous benefits, including anxiety relief, deep relaxation before sleep, and improved sleep quality. One of the advantages of guided bedtime meditations is their ability to help with anxiety relief. Young children often experience worries about bedtime, such as fear of the dark or monsters, as well as other irrational concerns which can make bedtime problematic.

Older children may experience anxiety for various reasons, such as school pressures or social interactions. Continually replaying these negative thoughts can make falling asleep quite difficult. Regardless of age, worry and anxiety can impact a child's overall well-being and affect their life on a daily basis.

The gentle guidance of meditations at bedtime teaches children how to visualize, focus on their breath, relax their bodies, and let go of worries. Over time, this practice helps them develop a sense of inner calm and resilience when faced with stressful situations while easing sleep anxiety and eliminating bedtime battles.

Moreover, guided meditations are invaluable for deep relaxation before sleep. In our fast-paced world, children are constantly surrounded by screens and overstimulation, making it challenging for them to wind down at the end of the day. Guided bedtime meditations offer a gentle transition from the day's hustle and bustle to a state of deep relaxation.

By guiding children through visualizations and soothing imagery, these meditations help them release tension and prepare their minds and bodies for the most tranquil sleep possible. One of the most significant benefits of guided bedtime meditations is their ability to enhance the quality of sleep our children are getting.

Mindful Magic

Many parents struggle with getting their little ones to settle down and sleep peacefully. What can be more stressful than constant bedtime bargaining and battles? Even once parents have gotten their kids to fall asleep, it is very common for a child to wake up periodically throughout the night in an attempt to continue to negotiate or manipulate the bedtime situation.

This effectively extends the battle, not only diminishing the quality of your child's sleep but also creating added stress and aggravation for parents. Bedtime battles are stressful for everyone and can even hinder a parent's ability to achieve restful sleep. The calming nature of guided meditations helps children relax their minds and bodies, preparing them for sound sleep.

By incorporating such meditations into their bedtime routine, parents can create a soothing environment that promotes a more peaceful and uninterrupted sleep for their children. Eliminating sleep battles makes bedtime a breeze and improves the quality of sleep for everyone, making bedtime meditations a win—win for all!

In conclusion, guided meditations for kids provide a myriad of benefits for children of all ages. With the addition of meditations into a consistent bedtime routine, parents can help their children relieve worries and anxiety, achieve deep relaxation, and experience improved sleep quality, while eliminating those frustrating bedtime battles.

As parents, it is our responsibility to empower our children with tools that support their emotional well-being, and guided meditations are a wonderful addition to any parent's toolkit.

Exploring the Science Behind Meditation and Sleep

In today's hectic, technology-driven world, it's no surprise that both children and adults struggle with getting a good night's sleep. As parents, we understand the importance of peaceful and restful sleep for our children's overall well-being and development, but let's dive into the science behind meditation and sleep.

Meditation has been practiced for centuries and is known to have numerous benefits for both the mind and body. But what exactly happens in the brain when we meditate? How does it promote better sleep? By exploring the science behind these practices, we can obtain a deeper understanding and empower ourselves to improve the quality of our children's sleep.

When we meditate, our brain enters a state of deep relaxation, reducing the production of stress hormones and increasing the release of "feel-good" chemicals such as serotonin and endorphins. This helps to calm the mind, ease anxiety, and promote a sense of overall well-being.

These benefits directly translate into better sleep quality. By incorporating meditation into their bedtime routine, you can help your child relax, let go of any worries or fears, and prepare their mind and body for a restful night's sleep.

In addition to the psychological benefits, there are also physiological changes that occur during meditation. Research has shown that meditation can lower heart rate, blood pressure, and cortisol levels, all of which contribute to a more peaceful and restorative sleep. By gaining an understanding of these scientific processes, you can confidently introduce meditation to your child as a tool for promoting healthy sleep patterns.

As parents, we want nothing more than to see our children happy, healthy, and well-rested. Through educating ourselves on the science behind meditation and sleep, we become equipped with the knowledge and tools to provide our children with the best possible sleep experience.

So join us on this journey into dreamland and discover the magic of meditation for peaceful sleep. Your child will thank you (someday) and you will witness the transformative power of a good night's sleep on their overall well-being.

Chapter 2

Getting Started with Bedtime Meditations

Creating a Soothing Atmosphere in the Bedroom

When it comes to bedtime, creating a peaceful environment in the bedroom is essential for helping your child have a restful and rejuvenating night's sleep. The bedroom should be a sanctuary, a place where they can feel safe, calm, and ready to drift off into dreamland. In this chapter, we will explore some valuable tips and techniques to create the perfect peaceful atmosphere in your child's bedroom.

First and foremost, it is helpful to declutter the space as much as possible. A cluttered room can be distracting, making it difficult for your child to settle down and relax, while a clutter-free environment promotes a calm and peaceful mind.

Try to keep the bedroom as tidy and organized as possible, creating a serene space for your child to relax. Encourage or help them to tidy up toys and books before bedtime, creating a serene environment that promotes tranquil thoughts.

Next, consider the lighting in the bedroom. Soft, dim lighting can create a cozy and tranquil ambiance. Avoid bright lights or harsh overhead lighting, as it can be stimulating and disrupt sleep. Instead, opt for warm and soothing nightlights, bedside lamps, or fairy lights to create a relaxing ambiance.

Another important aspect to consider is the color scheme. Choose soothing and calming colors for the bedroom walls, bedding, and curtains. Shades of blue, green, or pastel tones have a relaxing effect on the mind and help promote relaxation and tranquility to help your child unwind before sleep. Avoid bright and stimulating colors that can hinder sleep.

The temperature in the bedroom also plays a significant role in creating a peaceful atmosphere. Ensure that the room is neither too hot nor too cold, as extreme temperatures can disrupt sleep. Maintain a comfortable temperature that allows your child to snuggle up under their blankets and feel cozy.

Also consider including sensory items in the bedroom that promote relaxation, such as a lavender-scented diffuser or a sound machine playing calming nature sounds or gentle lullabies. These elements help to create a serene atmosphere conducive to deep relaxation. Allow your child to personalize their space with items that bring them comfort and make them happy.

Whether it's a favorite stuffed animal, a special blanket, or a cozy reading nook, these personal touches can help create a sense of security and calmness. Lastly, consider incorporating relaxation techniques into your child's bedtime routine. This can include soothing music, guided meditations, or bedtime stories that promote peace and tranquility.

By implementing these tips and techniques, you can create a serene atmosphere in your child's bedroom, setting the stage for a restful and rejuvenating sleep. Remember, a calm and tranquil environment is conducive to a good night's sleep, ensuring your child wakes up refreshed and ready for a new day of adventures.

Creating a Calm and Relaxing Bedtime Routine

Bedtime can often be a challenging time for both parents and children. As the day comes to an end, children's energy levels seem to spike, making it difficult for them to wind down and prepare for a good night's sleep. However, with the right bedtime routine, you can create a calm and peaceful atmosphere that promotes relaxation and helps your child drift into a peaceful slumber without fail.

Let's explore some strategies and techniques to establish a bedtime routine that will soothe nighttime worries and ensure a restful sleep for your child.

1. Set a Consistent Bedtime: Establishing a regular sleep schedule is crucial for children's overall well-being. Determine an appropriate bedtime for your child's age and stick to it every night. Consistency helps regulate their internal clock, making it easier for them to fall asleep and wake up refreshed.

2. Establish simple bedtime rituals that help your child transition from the busyness of the day to a peaceful state of mind. This could include brushing teeth, taking a warm bath, or enjoying a cup of herbal tea together. These rituals not only promote relaxation but also create a sense of security and predictability for your child.

3. Engage in mindful activities before bedtime to signal to your child's body that it's time to relax. Encourage reading a bedtime story together, practicing gentle stretching or yoga, or engaging in a quiet art or craft activity. Avoid stimulating activities such as screen time or rough play, as they can hinder the relaxation process.

4. Introduce your child to bedtime meditations to help calm the mind and relax the body, preparing them for sleep. This book offers a collection of dreamy bedtime meditation stories designed specifically for kids. Embark on sleepytime adventures that transport your child's imagination to serene and soothing places, easing their worries and helping them drift off to sleep.

By implementing these strategies and incorporating these bedtime meditation stories you will create a calming bedtime routine that will help your child achieve a restful and rejuvenating sleep. Remember, consistency and patience are essential, and soon enough, bedtime will become a cherished time of relaxation and connection between you and your child.

Addressing Bedtime Worries and Anxiety

As bedtime approaches, does it seem as though children's anxiety and fears begin to kick into full gear? As the day comes to an end, the imagination of young minds tends to run wild, often leading to nighttime anxiety.

These worries can range from monsters under the bed to fears of the dark or even separation anxiety. As parents, it's important to understand these concerns and find effective ways to address them, ensuring a peaceful and restful sleep for our little ones.

One common bedtime worry is the fear of monsters or imaginary creatures lurking in the dark corners of the room. To handle this fear, it is crucial to create a safe and comforting environment. Make sure the room is well-lit and provide a nightlight if necessary.

Engage your child in a discussion about their fears, acknowledging their feelings and explaining that monsters are a creation of their imagination and can't hurt them in real life. You can even involve your child in a fun activity like creating a "monster spray" using water and a few drops of essential oil, which they can use to banish any monsters from their room.

Separation anxiety is another worry that often arises at bedtime. Children may feel anxious about being away from their parents or loved ones, making it difficult for them to fall asleep. Establishing a consistent bedtime routine can help alleviate this worry.

Create a special bedtime ritual that involves cuddling, reading a story, or singing a lullaby. Reassure your child that you will be nearby and that they are safe. Consider leaving a comforting item, such as a stuffed animal or a family photo, in their bed to provide a sense of security.

The fear of the dark is another common bedtime worry that many children experience. To address this fear, gradually introduce the concept of darkness through play and storytelling during the day.

Use a nightlight or a soft lamp to create a gentle glow in your child's room. You can also introduce a bedtime meditation routine, like the ones found in this book to help your child relax and imagine peaceful, comforting scenes before drifting off to sleep.

Remember, patience and understanding are essential when handling bedtime worries. By addressing these concerns with empathy and implementing strategies that create a sense of security, you can help your child overcome their fears and enjoy a peaceful night's sleep.

Chapter
3

Mindfulness Techniques for Children

Nowadays, it's more important than ever to teach our children how to find moments of calmness and relaxation amidst the chaos of life. As parents, we want our children to feel safe, secure, and at peace, especially during bedtime.

That's why incorporating mindfulness into their nighttime routine can work wonders in helping them to fall asleep. In this chapter, we will review some simple, yet powerful mindfulness techniques to promote calmness and relaxation in children at bedtime, or any time.

Mindfulness Practices

1. Mindful Breathing: Breathing exercises are a fantastic way to introduce mindfulness to children of all ages. Encourage your child to take slow, deep breaths, focusing their attention on the sensation of the breath entering and leaving their body. This practice can help them relax and let go of any worries or anxieties.

2. Progressive Muscle Relaxation: This technique involves systematically tensing and releasing different muscle groups, promoting physical relaxation. It is particularly effective for children who struggle with anxiety or restlessness. Guide your child through a series of tensing and relaxing their muscles, starting from their toes and moving up to their head. By consciously releasing tension from their body, they can experience a reduction of anxiety levels and a sense of physical and mental relaxation.

3. Gratitude Journal: Introduce your child to the concept of gratitude by keeping a gratitude journal. Before bed, ask them to write or draw three things they are grateful for that day. This practice fosters a positive mindset and encourages them to appreciate the small joys in life.

4. Calming Music: Consider playing soft and tranquil melodies during your child's bedtime routine. Music has a calming effect on the nervous system, aiding in the transition from wakefulness to sleep.

5. Body Scan Meditation: Help your child become aware of their body and its sensations through a body scan meditation. Starting from their toes, guide them to focus on each body part, noticing any tension or discomfort. Encourage them to breathe into those areas and imagine the tension melting away.

6. Calming Sensory Activities: Incorporating calming sensory activities into the bedtime routine can be highly beneficial. Consider introducing activities such as a warm bath with lavender-scented bubbles, gentle massage with soothing oils, or listening to soft instrumental music. These activities can create a serene environment, promoting relaxation and tranquility.

7. Mindful Storytelling: Bedtime stories can be transformed into mindful experiences. Choose books that promote mindfulness, empathy, and emotional intelligence. As you read, pause to discuss the characters' emotions and encourage your child to reflect on how they would feel in similar situations.

8. Guided Imagery: Bedtime meditation stories are fantastic for achieving peaceful slumber. The magical meditations in this book take children to a world of imagination, where they can leave their worries behind. These guided stories engage their senses and help them focus on positive and calming imagery, easing their anxiety and inviting a restful sleep.

Keep in mind, consistency is important when establishing bedtime rituals. Aim to create a peaceful and predictable routine that your child can rely on. By choosing the right rituals and incorporating them into your child's routine, you can help them overcome anxiety, improve sleep quality, and promote relaxation and self-awareness. Remember, mindfulness is a lifelong skill, and starting early can have long-lasting benefits for your child's well-being.

Mindful Breathing Techniques

1. Belly Breathing: Teach your child to place one hand on their belly and take a deep breath in, feeling their belly rise like a balloon. Then, as they exhale, they can imagine their belly deflating. This technique helps slow down the breath, relax the body, and release tension.

2. 4-7-8 Breath: This technique involves inhaling for a count of 4, holding the breath for a count of 7, and exhaling slowly for a count of 8. Encourage your child to imagine their worries leaving their body with each exhale, creating space for calmness and relaxation.

3. Rainbow Breathing: Ask your child to imagine a beautiful rainbow in their mind. As they breathe in, they visualize the rainbow's colors filling their body with positive energy and calmness. As they breathe out, they imagine any stress or tension being released from their body.

4. Balloon Breathing: Have your child imagine they are holding a balloon in their hands. As they breathe in, they imagine the balloon expanding and filling with air. When they exhale, they visualize the balloon slowly deflating. This technique encourages deep, slow breaths and helps release any worries or anxious thoughts.

5. Starry Sky Breathing: Before bed, create a cozy atmosphere by dimming the lights and imagining a starry sky above (or a constellation projector if you have one). As your child lies down, guide them to take slow, deep breaths, imagining each breath connecting them with the peaceful energy of the stars. This technique promotes relaxation and a sense of tranquility.

By incorporating these breathing techniques into your child's bedtime routine, you can help them develop a sense of calmness, making it easier for them to fall asleep. Remember, practice makes perfect, so encourage your child to use these techniques regularly, even during moments of stress or anxiety throughout the day. Together, you and your child can set out on dreamland adventures, making bedtime something they look forward to each night.

Visualizations and Guided Imagery

Visualizations are a wonderful tool that can transport children to magical places and create a sense of calmness and relaxation before bedtime. By engaging their imagination, visualizations can help children release anxiety, stress, and worries, allowing them to drift off and sleep peacefully.

Guided imagery is a proven method that uses visualization to promote relaxation and create a calm state of mind. Through this process, children can travel to a tranquil place where worries and stress melt away without even leaving their bedrooms. Through the power of storytelling and soothing words, we can guide our little ones into a restful slumber.

Bedtime meditations are highly effective in preparing children for a peaceful night's sleep. Through soothing and gentle guidance, meditations can help your child relax their body and mind, leading to improved sleep quality.

By incorporating guided imagery and visualizations into meditations, we are able to offer a structured approach to winding down, creating a peaceful sanctuary that is conducive to sleep where children can feel safe, loved, and at peace.

Guided meditations can also be a powerful tool to alleviate anxiety. By guiding your child through a calming visualization, they can learn to let go of their worries and fears. Imagine your child visualizing themselves floating on a soft, fluffy cloud, gently drifting away from any anxious thoughts or feelings.

Such relaxing imagery can help ease their anxiety and promote a sense of tranquility, making it easier for them to fall asleep and stay asleep throughout the night. Sleep meditation for anxiety relief is essential for children who struggle with racing thoughts or have difficulty unwinding at bedtime.

By using visualizations that focus on slow, deep breathing and the release of tension, your child can experience a deep sense of calmness before sleep. They can visualize their body becoming loose and limp, releasing any tension or stress that may be holding them back from achieving restful sleep.

Bedtime meditations are designed to enhance the overall sleep experience. Through visualizations of calming scenes, such as a peaceful beach or a serene forest, your child can create a mental space that promotes relaxation and tranquility. By engaging their senses and guiding them through these visualizations, your child's mind can become still, allowing them to drift off into a deep and restorative sleep.

Meditations before sleep are particularly beneficial for children who struggle with hyperactivity or restlessness at bedtime. Through visualizations that focus on stillness and tranquility, your child can learn to quiet their mind and body, preparing them for rest. Imagining themselves as a gentle stream flowing calmly through a beautiful meadow, for example, can help them feel grounded and at peace, paving the way for a tranquil night's sleep.

Incorporating meditations utilizing visualizations and guided imagery into your child's bedtime routine can be a game-changer in promoting quality sleep. By creating a calming and peaceful environment through guided meditations, your child can experience deep relaxation, anxiety relief, and improved sleep quality.

So, get ready to embark on a magical journey with your child, where dreams are peaceful, worries are left behind, and a tranquil sleep filled with peaceful dreams awaits.

Chapter
4

Engaging Parent-Child Bonding through Bedtime Meditations

The Role of Affection and Connection in Meditation Practices

Who ever said that meditation is just for adults? It can be incredibly beneficial for children as well, helping them develop focus, manage their emotions, and find inner peace. However, one aspect that is often overlooked in meditation practices is the role of affection and connection.

Sure, the power of mindfulness and meditation will work their magic and get your children sleeping peacefully in no time, but what parent wouldn't want to enjoy a bit more affection and connection with their child? Incorporating affection and connection into children's meditation practices will take their bedtime routine to the next level.

Affection and connection are fundamental human needs, and they play a significant role in fostering a sense of safety and security. When children feel loved and connected, they are more likely to be open to new experiences and embrace the practice of meditation.

During your child's bedtime routine, parents are encouraged to create a loving and nurturing environment by holding their child's hand, giving them a gentle hug, or simply sitting close to them. These simple gestures can have a profound impact on their overall experience.

Furthermore, incorporating affection and connection into meditation practices helps children develop a positive relationship with their own emotions. By providing a safe space for them to explore their feelings, they learn to acknowledge and accept them without judgment. This allows them to develop emotional resilience and cope better with challenges they may face in their daily lives.

In addition to fostering emotional well-being, affection and connection at bedtime can also promote better sleep. The soothing presence of a parent and the feeling of being loved and cared for help children relax and drift into a peaceful slumber. Incorporating these elements into your bedtime routine enables you to create a magical experience that not only helps children fall asleep but also leaves them feeling secure, loved, and at peace.

In conclusion, the role of affection and connection in meditation practices cannot be overstated. This addition to your bedtime routine provides children with a nurturing and loving environment where they can explore their emotions, find inner peace, and experience restful sleep.

As parents, let us embrace the power of affection and connection and guide our children on their journey of self-discovery and emotional well-being. Kids don't stay young for very long and will be teenagers before you know it so take advantage of the opportunity to cuddle and connect with them now, while they still allow you into their bedrooms!

Fostering Positive Communication and Mindful Listening

In the world we live in today, fostering positive communication and mindful listening has become more important than ever, especially when it comes to our children. As parents, we play a crucial role in shaping our kids' communication skills and teaching them the value of attentive listening. Let's review some practical tips and strategies to enhance your child's communication abilities and nurture a peaceful and harmonious environment at home.

First and foremost, we will explore the importance of modeling positive communication. Children learn by observing their parents, and if they see respectful and effective communication between adults, they are more likely to emulate it. Strategies such as active listening, expressing emotions constructively, and resolving conflicts peacefully are helpful in promoting effective communication skills.

Another helpful communication strategy is mindful listening, which involves being fully present and attentive when someone else is speaking. Mindful listening is key to good communication development, with many benefits, such as improved understanding, enhanced empathy, and strengthened relationships, in which open and honest communication between you and your child is encouraged.

By fostering positive communication and mindful listening, you will not only improve your child's communication skills but also create a safe and nurturing environment for them to express their emotions and thoughts. Together, we can transform bedtime into a special experience that will, not only help your child sleep, but also strengthen your bond and create lasting memories.

Chapter
5

Empowering Children with Self-Meditation Techniques

Teaching Children Self-Meditation Skills

Teaching children self-meditation is a valuable skill that can, not only help them to have a restful sleep and wake up refreshed and ready for the day ahead, it can benefit them throughout their lives. Self-meditation is a practice that allows children to create a calm and serene space within themselves. It helps them to quiet their minds, let go of worries, and experience a sense of inner peace.

By incorporating self-meditation into their bedtime routine, children can find comfort and relaxation, making it easier for them to fall asleep at night. One of the most effective ways to introduce self-meditation to children is through the use of bedtime meditation stories.

Meditations such as the enchanting tales in this book will transport children to a world of wonder and imagination, guiding them on relaxing sleepytime adventures. Through these stories, children can embark on a journey that soothes their nighttime worries and anxieties, allowing them to let go and unwind.

Each meditation story will engage children's senses and capture their imagination. As parents, we can read these stories to our children or play guided meditation recordings that inspire them to imagine themselves in the magical worlds described.

By following along with the story and engaging in simple mindfulness exercises, children learn to focus their attention, let go of distractions, and find a sense of calm. It's important to remember that teaching self-meditation skills to children is a gradual process.

It is essential to start with short and simple meditation sessions, gradually increasing the duration as your child becomes more comfortable. Consistency is key, so incorporating self-meditation into your child's bedtime routine every night can help establish a sense of familiarity and make it easier for them to relax.

By teaching children self-meditation skills, we empower them with a lifelong tool for managing stress and finding inner peace. We, as parents, play a vital role in guiding our children towards a restful sleep and a peaceful mind. The magical bedtime meditation stories in this book provide a wonderful resource for parents of young children to introduce their little ones to the world of self-meditation and create a soothing and relaxing bedtime routine while building self-awareness and regulation skills that will last them a lifetime.

Encouraging Children to Express Their Emotions

One of the most important skills we can teach our children is how to express their emotions effectively. In this busy, world, with all its pressures, it can be easy for kids to feel overwhelmed and unsure of how to communicate their feelings. As parents, it is our responsibility to provide them with the tools and support they need to express themselves in a healthy and constructive way.

So, how can we encourage our children to express their emotions? Here are a few strategies that can help:

1. Create a safe and judgment-free environment: Let your children know that it is okay to feel and express their emotions. Create a safe space where they feel comfortable sharing their thoughts and feelings without fear of judgment or punishment.

2. Listen actively: When your child opens up about their emotions, be an active listener. Give them your full attention, maintain eye contact, and show genuine interest in what they have to say. This will make them feel valued and understood.

3. Teach them emotional vocabulary: Help your children expand their emotional vocabulary by using descriptive words to label different emotions. This will enable them to better understand and express their feelings.

4. Lead by example: Children often learn by observing their parents' behavior. Model healthy emotional expression by sharing your own feelings and demonstrating effective coping strategies when faced with challenging situations.

5. Offer alternative outlets: Encourage your children to express their emotions through various outlets such as art, music, or writing. These creative activities can provide a safe and constructive way for them to process and communicate their feelings.

Remember, encouraging your children to express their emotions is an ongoing process. Be patient and understanding as they navigate this journey of self-discovery. By providing them with the necessary tools and support, you are helping them develop essential emotional skills that will benefit them throughout their lives.

Chapter 6

Fun Activities to Support Bedtime Meditations

One of the most wonderful experiences of childhood is the world of dreams. The imagination of children knows no bounds, and their dreams often take them on incredible adventures. As parents, we want to encourage and celebrate these magical moments with our children.

One way to do this is by engaging them in bedtime crafts and activities that honor and acknowledge their dreams. Let's explore a few activities that can be introduced to children, either as part of their bedtime routine or at any time, in order to motivate them to get to dreaming.

Crafting Dreamcatchers for Sweet Dreams

Dreamcatchers have long been a symbol of protection and positive energy in Native American culture, believed to filter out bad dreams and let only good dreams pass through. The art of crafting dreamcatchers is a wonderful activity for parents and children to bond over while creating a magical tool for sweet dreams.

Materials needed:

- A hoop (can be made from wire, embroidery hoop, or even a suitable branch)
- String or yarn
- Beads, ribbons, feathers, or any decorative items of choice
- Scissors

Step 1: Prepare the hoop

Start by choosing the size of the dreamcatcher you want to create. You can use a ready-made hoop or craft your own using wire or a branch. The hoop represents the circle of life and the unity of all things.

Step 2: Weave the web

Take your string or yarn and tie one end securely to the hoop. Begin weaving the string in a spiral motion around the hoop, gradually moving towards the center. Leave some gaps in the web, as these are believed to let good dreams pass through. As you weave, encourage your child to imagine positive thoughts and intentions for a peaceful sleep.

Step 3: Add decorative elements

Once the web is complete, it's time to add some decorative elements. Let your child's creativity shine by choosing beads, ribbons, feathers, or any other items they find appealing. These elements not only add beauty to the dreamcatcher but also enhance its protective and positive energy.

Step 4: Hang and activate:

Find a special place in your child's bedroom to hang the dreamcatcher. It can be above their bed or near a window, where it can catch the morning light. Before hanging it, take a moment with your child to activate the dreamcatcher's power.

Guide them to close their eyes, hold the dreamcatcher in their hands, and imagine it glowing with positive energy. Guide them to visualize it creating a shield around them, protecting them from bad dreams, and inviting only sweet dreams into their sleep.

Step 5: Sweet dreams ahead

Encourage your child to interact with their dreamcatcher before bedtime. They can gently touch it, whisper their wishes, or simply admire its beauty. Remind them that their dreamcatcher is there to watch over them, ensuring a restful night's sleep filled with pleasant dreams.

Crafting dreamcatchers not only engages your child's creativity but also serves as a symbolic tool for promoting peaceful and positive sleep. Enjoy this activity together and watch your child drift off to dreamland with a sense of calm and security. Sweet dreams await!

Creating Dream Journals to Capture Magical Moments

Dream journals are a fantastic tool for capturing and preserving the memories of your child's dreams. They provide a space for children to express their creativity and reflect on their nighttime adventures. Not only will this activity foster their imagination, but it will also encourage mindfulness and self-reflection.

To start, you'll need a notebook or a special journal dedicated solely to dreams. Involve your child in selecting the journal; they'll be more excited about using it if they have a say in choosing one that speaks to their personality. Encourage them to decorate it with stickers, drawings, or anything else that sparks their imagination.

Next, set aside a few minutes each morning to sit down with your child and discuss their dreams. Ask them to describe the places they visited, the characters they encountered, and the emotions they felt.

Encourage them to use their senses and be as descriptive as possible. You can even suggest that they draw pictures of their dreams to bring them to life. As your child shares their dreams, write them down in the dream journal. This will help them solidify their memory and allow you to revisit these magical moments together in the future.

Not only will this activity promote bonding between you and your child, but it will also help them develop their storytelling skills and improve their writing abilities. Additionally, encourage your child to reflect on their dreams and what they might mean. Ask open-ended questions to prompt their thinking, such as "Why do you think you dreamed about that?" or "How did your dream make you feel?" This will help them develop a deeper understanding of their emotions and thoughts.

Creating dream journals is a beautiful way to celebrate and honor your child's imagination. It allows them to explore the depths of their dreams, fostering creativity, self-expression, and mindfulness. As you engage in this process together, your child will come to treasure their dream journal as a magical keepsake of their nighttime adventures.

Playing Relaxing Music for Peaceful Sleep

Music has a unique way of soothing our minds and bodies, and it can have a profound impact on our sleep quality. When we listen to calming melodies, our brain releases serotonin, a hormone that helps us relax and feel at ease. This is particularly beneficial for children who may have trouble falling asleep due to nighttime worries or fears.

By incorporating relaxing music into your child's bedtime routine, you can create a tranquil environment that promotes restful sleep. The soft melodies and gentle rhythms will help lull them into a state of relaxation, allowing their minds to let go of any stress or anxiety accumulated throughout the day.

One of the best genres of music to play during bedtime is instrumental, as it lacks lyrics that may stimulate the brain and keep it active. Choose soothing melodies that feature gentle instruments like the piano, flute, or soft guitar. These calming sounds will create a serene atmosphere, perfect for sleepytime.

To maximize the benefits of playing relaxing music, consider using specialized playlists or albums designed specifically for bedtime. These collections often feature compositions that are scientifically proven to induce relaxation and improve sleep quality. Look for albums labeled as "sleep music" or "calming lullabies" to ensure you choose the most suitable music for your child.

Remember to adjust the volume to a comfortable level, ensuring it is not too loud or too soft. The music should act as a soothing background noise rather than overpowering the room. Additionally, set a timer to automatically stop the music after a certain period, so it doesn't disrupt your child's sleep once they have drifted off.

By incorporating the magic of relaxing music into your child's bedtime routine, you can create a peaceful and soothing environment that will help them drift into a restful slumber. Sweet dreams await as you embark on this dreamy adventure of bedtime meditation and relaxation.

Mindful Magic

Dreamy Bedtime Meditations for Children

We hope you're enjoying
Dreamy Bedtime Meditations for Children.
It's through your support and reviews that this book is able to reach the hands, minds, and hearts
of more parents and children.
Please kindly take a moment to leave a review on
Amazon. Please scan the QR code below.
If you reside in a country that isn't listed, please use the link provided in your Amazon order.

Please follow these simple steps to leave a review for this book:
1. Open the camera on your phone
2. Hover it over the QR code below
3. Leave a review once you're taken to the appropriate page

All it takes is a minute to make a difference.
Thank you for your support!

Chapter 7

Maintaining Consistency and Forming Lasting Habits

The Importance of Consistency

When it comes to promoting peaceful sleep and helping children navigate nighttime worries, consistency is key. Consistency in bedtime meditations provides a sense of security and familiarity for children. By establishing a regular meditation practice, you create a predictable routine that signals to your child's brain that it is time to wind down and prepare for sleep.

This uniformity helps to regulate their internal body clock, making it easier for them to fall asleep and wake up at consistent times each day. Furthermore, consistent bedtime meditations can help children develop a sense of mindfulness and self-awareness. By engaging in guided meditation stories night after night, they learn to focus their attention, regulate their emotions, and connect with their inner selves.

This mindfulness practice carries over into their daily lives, enhancing their overall well-being and emotional resilience. Consistency also reinforces the power of meditation as a tool for relaxation and stress reduction. When children experience the soothing effects of meditation consistently, they begin to associate it with a sense of calm and tranquility. This association helps them to naturally relax and let go of any worries or anxieties that may be keeping them awake at night.

Additionally, consistent bedtime meditations strengthen the parent-child bond. By engaging in these peaceful rituals together, parents create a special time for connection and nurturing. This shared experience promotes feelings of safety and love, cultivating a sense of trust between parent and child.

To ensure consistency in your child's bedtime meditations, establish a regular routine. Set a designated time each night to begin your bedtime routine, ensuring enough time to wind down and be ready for meditation. Create a cozy and quiet environment, free from distractions, and then let the magic of the meditations take over.

Tips for Staying Consistent with Bedtime Meditations

These magical practices not only promote restful sleep but also help children develop emotional intelligence and self-awareness. However, staying consistent with bedtime meditations can be a bit tricky, so here are some tips to help parents establish a bedtime routine that includes dreamy meditation stories:

1. Create a Calm and Cozy Environment: Designate a special space in your child's room for bedtime meditations. Make it cozy and inviting by adding soft blankets, pillows, and dim lighting to set the mood for relaxation.

2. Set a Consistent Bedtime: Establishing a regular bedtime routine is crucial for helping children wind down. Consistency sends signals to their brains that it's time to relax and prepare for sleep. Make sure to allocate enough time for meditation before their designated bedtime.

3. Choose Age-Appropriate Meditation Stories: Find meditation stories that are tailored to your child's age group. This book offers meditation stories specifically designed for children ages 4-10. These enchanting tales will captivate their imaginations and guide them into a state of tranquility.

4. Make it a Family Affair: Encourage siblings or the whole family to participate in bedtime meditations. This not only creates a sense of togetherness but also helps children feel more comfortable and engaged in the practice.

5. Consistency is Key: Consistency is vital when it comes to establishing any routine, including bedtime meditations. Try to incorporate this practice into your child's nightly routine and stick to it as much as possible. Consistency will reinforce the importance of relaxation and help your child form a habit of peaceful bedtime rituals.

6. Practice Patience: Some nights, your child might not feel like meditating or might find it challenging to settle down. Be patient and understanding during these moments. Gently remind them of the benefits of meditation and the magical adventures that await them in their dreams.

Dreamy Bedtime Meditations for Children

By establishing a regular routine and engaging in guided meditation stories night after night, you provide your child with a sense of security, mindfulness, relaxation, and a strengthened parent-child bond. Embrace the magic of consistent bedtime meditations and watch as your child peacefully drifts off into dreamland.

Chapter
8

Guided Bedtime Meditations

Join us on this magical journey through Mindful Magic, and watch as your child's worries and nighttime anxieties are gently swept away, leaving only peace and serenity in their wake. Let the power of these dreamy meditation stories guide your child into a restful slumber and ensure they wake up feeling refreshed and ready for a brand new day.

Remember, dear parents, that the power of guided meditation lies in its ability to harness the imagination and transport children to a place of tranquility. Be sure to incorporate these meditations into your child's bedtime routine so you can create a peaceful and soothing bedtime experience that promotes deep and restful sleep.

Guided Meditation: Cloud Dreaming

Once upon a bright and sunny day, as the gentle breeze caresses the earth, you find yourself nestled cozily in your bed, ready for a magical journey. Take a deep breath, close your eyes, and imagine yourself lying in the grass looking up at the big blue sky filled with soft, fluffy clouds. Find the biggest, fluffiest cloud you can find, and as you watch that cloud, notice as it begins to float, very slowly down to you.

But this is no ordinary cloud. It's a magic cloud that has the power to take you on wondrous journeys of enchantment. The cloud floats all the way down and lands right in front of you so you're able to just climb onto it. Let yourself relax into the soft, fluffy cloud and feel your body sink down cozily into it.

You can even wrap the cloud around you and snuggle down into it like a soft, billowy blanket. You immediately feel a sense of calm and security and you know that you are safe and protected wherever you go. The cloud cradles you gently, and you feel weightless as it begins to float.

Mindful Magic

As your cloud begins its journey, you feel it lifting you ever so gently, higher and higher. As you look down, you can see the world below getting smaller and smaller as your cloud floats you higher and higher. Trees and buildings appear like miniature toys and the rivers meander like silver ribbons.

You're soaring way up higher and higher. Birds fly by you as you float on your cloud, embraced by the vastness of the boundless blue sky. The sun smiles warmly upon you as your cloud drifts higher. You feel the sun's gentle rays kiss your cheeks, bringing a sense of comfort and happiness.

You bask in the warmth, feeling like a tiny star amidst the vast sky. Drifting and floating. Floating and drifting. As your cloud continues its journey, you find yourself passing through a field of fluffy clouds. They feel like soft cotton candy, and you delight in their sweet embrace. The air is filled with a faint scent of vanilla and rainbows, and you breathe it in, feeling the sweetness fill your lungs.

As you drift higher, you encounter a friendly flock of birds soaring nearby. They chirp and sing, inviting you to join in their harmonious melody. You join the chorus, feeling the music resonate through your being, lifting your spirits to new heights. Drifting and floating. Floating and drifting.

The cloud carries you to a place where the sky becomes a canvas of colors. It's a celestial painting, with shades of pink, orange, and lavender blending together like an artist's brushstrokes. You watch the colors dance and swirl, feeling a sense of peace wash over you.

You come across a magical rainbow stretching across the sky. Its colors shimmer and shift, creating a mesmerizing display of light. You reach out and feel the cool, silky touch of the rainbow and it leaves sparkling stardust on your fingers.

Next, your cloud takes you to a place where the wind whispers secrets through the sky. You lean into the breeze, feeling its gentle caress against your skin. The wind carries messages of love and encouragement, reminding you that you are special and loved.

As you continue your journey, Drifting and floating. Floating and drifting, you encounter a family of playful clouds. They have shapes like fluffy animals and smiling faces. They invite you to play hide-and-seek among them, and you giggle with delight, feeling like you've made new cloud friends.

The cloud guides you to a place where rainbows arch across the sky like bridges to distant lands. You walk along the rainbow, feeling the colors beneath your feet. You imagine where each color might lead, and the possibilities feel endless.

As the day turns to dusk, the cloud carries you to a spot where the stars begin to twinkle like tiny diamonds. The night sky is like a magical theater, with stars putting on a celestial show. You lie back on your cloud, watching shooting stars streak across the sky like fireworks. You float along watching the light show above as the stars zip and zoom through the heavens. Zipping and zooming. Zooming and zipping.

Your cloud leads you to a serene stretch of sky where the moon smiles down upon you. It's a gentle, silver crescent that radiates tranquility. You feel the moon's calming energy as it cradles you in its glow. As your cloud floats on, you find yourself at the moon's playground, where lunar craters look like giant puddles waiting to be splashed in.

You hop and leap, feeling the moon's low gravity making you so light on your feet, you're practically flying. You giggle and laugh, feeling the joy of being weightless and carefree. Hopping and leaping. Leaping and hopping.

With the night deepening, the cloud guides you back to your cozy bed. You lie down on the cloud, feeling its softness embrace you like a warm hug. Never before have you felt so relaxed and peaceful, Your eyelids are feeling so heavy, it's difficult to keep them open.

You feel like you could drift off to sleep at any moment. The stars bid you goodnight, and the moon sends you dreams of wonder and joy. Your cloud begins to descend and you feel yourself floating down ever so gently.

You're drifting and floating lower and lower until your cloud reaches your room and lands you softly onto your bed. Your body feels so heavy, you could sink right through the bed, into a world of dreams and imagination. You drift off gently, into a peaceful slumber as the magic of the cloud lulls you into a realm of serenity, where your heart can soar and your mind can rest.

Sleep tight, dear child, and may the cloud always carry you to dreamy adventures in the sky. Goodnight.

Guided Meditation: Starlight Voyage

Once upon a twinkling night, as the moon illuminates the velvety sky, you find yourself nestled cozily in your bed, ready for a magical journey. Take a deep breath, close your eyes, and imagine yourself sitting by the window. The night sky is sprinkled with shimmering stars that twinkle and dance across the darkness.

As you gaze out the window upon the night sky, look for the biggest, brightest star you can find. This is no ordinary star. This is a magical star that can take you on bedtime adventures.

Now watch that star as it begins to move closer and closer toward your window. The star is growing bigger and brighter as it shoots across the night sky, making its way right to you. The star slows down as it approaches and stops right in front of your window, illuminating everything with its warm, radiant glow. The star greets you and invites you to climb aboard for the most peaceful and amazing adventure you could ever imagine.

The star moves even closer to your window so you can just climb right onto it. Its magic forms a protective screen that keeps its heat inside, while you remain nice and comfortable on the surface as you nestle into its cozy warmth.

You instantly feel so loved and safe, you know you will be protected and comforted wherever you go. The star cradles you gently, and you feel weightless as it begins to glide. As your star takes flight, you look down and see the world below. The star begins to carry you higher and higher, carrying you further up into the sky.

Your star soars through the vast night sky and up, up, up into outer space. Lights twinkle like fairy dust and the city below sparkles like a magical kingdom. You're soaring with the stars, embraced by the enchantment of the night.

The star's soft glow illuminates your path, and you find yourself passing through clusters of stardust. The stardust sparkles like tiny diamonds, and you reach out to touch it, feeling its warmth against your fingertips. As your star ascends higher and higher, you encounter a group of friendly fireflies.

They fly beside you, their lights flickering like tiny lanterns. They lead you to a hidden meadow of lavender clouds, where you lie down on what feels like soft bushy lavender. The fireflies create a mesmerizing light show, filling the meadow with a magical glow. Your star carries you. Gliding and soaring. Soaring and gliding.

Mindful Magic

The star takes you to a place where the moon's reflection dances on a tranquil sky lake. The water shimmers like silver silk, and you dip your hand in, feeling the coolness on your skin. The moon's reflection smiles back at you, as if inviting you to take a moonlit boat ride.

Next, your star carries you to a celestial garden in outer space. The garden is filled with blooming stars in every color imaginable. You walk among them, feeling their gentle light caress your skin. Their soft glow creates a peaceful ambiance, and you feel like you've entered a realm of dreams.

As you continue your journey, you come across a group of shooting stars streaking across the sky. They zoom and swirl, leaving trails of stardust in their wake. You make a wish upon each shooting star, feeling the magic of the universe enveloping you as you continue along. Gliding and soaring. Soaring and gliding.

The star guides you to a place where constellations form ancient stories in the night sky. You trace the lines with your fingers, listening to the tales whispered by the stars. The stories fill your heart with wonder and curiosity, as you imagine exploring distant galaxies and meeting cosmic beings.

As the night deepens, the star leads you through a cosmic storm of colors. Nebulas swirl like majestic paint strokes, creating a celestial canvas of breathtaking beauty. You feel the energy of the universe surrounding you, and you're filled with a sense of awe and gratitude as you continue on this magical journey. Gliding and soaring. Soaring and gliding.

The star carries you to a tranquil comet shower, where comets streak through the sky like shooting stars on a grand scale. You watch in amazement as they light up the night, leaving trails of brilliance behind them. With the night at its peak, the star takes you on a journey beyond the boundaries of space and time.

You soar among distant planets and dance with swirling galaxies. You feel connected to the vastness of the cosmos, knowing that you are a part of something much greater than yourself.

You soak up the brilliance of this incredible universe that you are a part of. Gliding and soaring. Soaring and gliding. The star begins to gently drift downward and you feel yourself being rocked ever so softly as you soar back down, down, down. You feel your body getting so heavy, it feels like your weight is pulling the star down. You can see the houses and trees getting closer and closer as your star descends back down to Earth.

Mindful Magic

It carries you right back to your window and gently guides you back to your cozy bed. As you snuggle into bed, feeling its softness embrace you like a warm hug, your eyelids feel so heavy you can barely keep your eyes open. The constellations bid you goodnight, and the moon sends you dreams of celestial wonders and cosmic adventures. You drift off into a peaceful slumber, and smile, knowing your star is soaring through the night sky and outer space, as you glide into a world of dreams and boundless possibilities.

The magic of the star lulls you into a realm of tranquility, where your imagination can soar and your spirit can rest. Sleep tight, dear child, and may the star always carry you to dreamy adventures among the stars and beyond. Goodnight.

Guided Meditation: The Enchanted Forest

Once upon a moonlit night, as the stars twinkle like fairy lights in the sky, you find yourself nestled cozily in your bed, ready for a magical adventure. Take a deep breath, close your eyes, and imagine yourself walking along a hidden path. As you follow along the path, you notice a forest filled with tall trees ahead in the distance. Each step you take leads you closer to the trees and as you approach them you realize you are entering a magical forest.

The air is filled with the scent of moss and wildflowers, and you feel a sense of wonder and excitement in your heart. As you venture deeper and deeper into the forest, the trees seem to whisper ancient secrets, and the leaves rustle like a soothing melody. The magic of the forest surrounds you like a warm embrace, and you feel safe and at ease in this enchanted realm.

You can feel the love that surrounds you from every direction, wrapping you up in it just like a warm, cozy blanket and you know you are safe and protected wherever you go.

Mindful Magic

As you continue on your journey, you come across a gentle stream that weaves through the forest. The water glistens like liquid silver, and you dip your fingers into the cool, refreshing flow. You feel the water's calming touch as it washes away any worries or fears, leaving you with a sense of peace and calm.

The forest comes alive with friendly creatures. You encounter playful rabbits hopping among the ferns, and you follow a family of squirrels as they chase each other up the trees. The forest animals welcome you to their magical home, and you feel a sense of belonging and connection with the natural world.

Next, you find yourself in a sunlit glade, where colorful butterflies flit about like living rainbows. Their delicate wings brush against your skin, and you feel a tingling sensation of joy. The butterflies invite you to join in their dance, and you twirl and spin among them, feeling light and carefree. Twirling and spinning. Spinning and twirling.

As the day turns to dusk, the forest begins to glow with soft, twinkling lights. The fireflies come out to play, and their tiny lanterns light up the night like stars on the forest floor. You lie down on a bed of moss, watching the fireflies dance in the night sky, and you feel a sense of wonder and enchantment. as they flit back and forth, dancing around you. Flitting and dancing. Dancing and flitting.

The forest leads you to a majestic tree, whose branches reach out toward the sky like outstretched arms. This is the Heartwood Tree, the guardian of the magic forest. You place your hand on the tree's trunk, feeling its ancient wisdom and the pulse of the forest's energy. It whispers to you, reminding you that you are loved and protected.

The forest takes you to a place where the trees part to reveal a shimmering waterfall. The water cascades down in a gentle flow, creating a soothing sound that fills the air. You sit by the waterfall, feeling its mist kiss your cheeks, and you close your eyes, letting the water's melody lull you into a state of deep relaxation.

As you continue your journey, you come across a hidden pond with water so clear it reflects the stars above. The pond is like a mirror to the universe, and you gaze into its depths, feeling a sense of oneness with all of creation. You see the stars twinkling in the water, and you imagine yourself floating among them, becoming a part of the cosmic dance. Floating and twinkling. Twinkling and floating.

The forest leads you to a clearing where a gentle breeze carries the scent of blooming flowers. You lie down on the soft grass, feeling the earth's energy beneath you. The breeze kisses your cheeks, and you close your eyes, feeling completely at peace.

With the night deepening, the forest invites you to rest under a canopy of leaves. The trees above form a natural dome, creating a sanctuary of tranquility. You snuggle into your cozy bed, feeling the embrace of the forest's magic around you. You feel your body becoming so heavy, you could sink right down through your bed. You can't even manage to stay awake a moment longer.

As you drift off into a peaceful slumber, the forest whispers its lullaby in your ears, guiding you to dreamy adventures among the trees and stars. The magic of the forest lulls you into a realm of serenity, where your imagination can roam free and your heart can find solace.

Sleep tight, dear child, and may the enchanted forest always be there to welcome you to dreamland. Goodnight.

Guided Meditation: Deep Sea Adventure

Once upon a starry night, as the moon smiles down from above, you find yourself nestled comfortably in your cozy bed, ready for a magical journey. Close your eyes, take a deep breath, and imagine yourself on a sandy beach by the ocean's edge. The waves gently lapping the shore are like a soothing lullaby, and you feel safe and secure in this dreamy world.

As you gaze out at the sparkling sea, you notice a mystical submarine emerging from the depths of the water. Its exterior is adorned with colorful patterns and friendly sea creatures who welcome you aboard for a magical undersea adventure.

You climb aboard with excitement bubbling in your heart and you instantly have the feeling of love surrounding you from every direction, wrapping you in a soft cozy blanket. You know you are safe and protected wherever you go.

Inside the submarine, you meet the captain, a kind and wise seafarer, who welcomes you warmly, assuring you that this journey will be filled with wonder and joy. The submarine's cabin is cozy, with soft cushions and twinkling lights that resemble stars in the night sky.

Mindful Magic

The submarine begins to descend into the deep blue sea, and you watch in awe as sunlight filters through the water, creating a mesmerizing dance of colors. As you plunge down deeper, deeper, deeper through the ocean the world outside the portholes transforms into a magical undersea kingdom. Coral reefs stretch as far as the eye can see, and fish of all shapes and sizes swim gracefully by.

You begin to feel weightless and calm as the submarine glides smoothly through the water. The captain encourages you to peer outside the porthole and marvel at the wonders of the sea. Schools of playful dolphins accompany the submarine, leaping and twirling as if they're putting on a show just for you. Leaping and twirling. Twirling and leaping.

Next, you spot a group of sea turtles gracefully gliding through the water. Their serene presence reminds you to take deep breaths, just like they do when they rise to the surface for air. You inhale slowly, feeling the coolness of the sea air filling your lungs, and then exhale, releasing any remaining tension from your body.

Further along, the submarine approaches a magnificent coral garden. The corals come in all colors of the rainbow, and they look like a breathtaking underwater city. Tiny fish dart in and out of the corals, playing hide-and-seek with you, making you laugh and giggle with delight.

The captain gently steers the submarine through an underwater cave adorned with sparkling crystals. The cave feels like a secret sanctuary, a place of pure peace and tranquility. You close your eyes and take a moment to listen to the gentle hum of the submarine and the faint sounds of the ocean outside, feeling completely at ease.

As you continue your journey, you come across a sunken ship, now home to a curious octopus family. They wave their tentacles at you, inviting you to join their dance. You sway along, feeling the soothing rhythm of the sea guiding your movements as if you're dancing with the water itself. Dancing and twirling. Twirling and dancing.

The submarine takes you deeper into the sea, where you discover a hidden grotto filled with glowing jellyfish. Their soft light illuminates the surroundings, creating a mesmerizing display of colors. You feel a sense of wonder and awe at the beauty of nature as you watch them gliding and drifting through the sea outside. Gliding and drifting. Drifting and gliding.

As the journey nears its end, the submarine starts ascending up, up, up back toward the surface. The sea creatures bid you farewell with twinkling eyes and gentle waves. You feel grateful for the incredible adventure you've had, and a warm sense of joy and contentment fills your heart. The submarine reaches the surface and the sandy beach appears through the porthole at the water's edge.

Mindful Magic

You step back onto the sandy beach and say goodbye to the captain, thankful for this enchanting journey. You climb back into your cozy bed, feeling relaxed and at peace. Your body feels so heavy, you could sink right through it. The memories of the undersea adventure bring a smile to your face and your eyes roll back in your head as you drift off into a serene slumber, surrounded by the calming presence of the ocean in your dreams.

Sleep tight, dear child, and embrace the magic of the sea in your heart. Goodnight.

Guided Meditation: The Magical Garden

Once upon a moonlit night, as the stars twinkled in the velvety sky, you find yourself lying cozily in your bed, ready to embark on a magical adventure. Take a deep breath, close your eyes, and imagine yourself walking along a winding path through a lush forest. The air is filled with the sweet scent of blooming flowers, and you feel a gentle breeze brushing against your cheeks.

As you stroll deeper into the forest, the trees open their branches to reveal a hidden gateway adorned with sparkling crystals. This is the entrance to the magical garden, a place where magic comes alive. As you step slowly through the gateway, you find yourself in a world of wonder and enchantment.

The magical garden is like no other. It's filled with plants and flowers of every color imaginable. Each flower seems to radiate its own soft glow, casting a gentle luminescence over the entire garden. You feel safe and protected in this magical oasis.

As you wander through the garden, you come across a babbling brook. The water glistens with an ethereal light, and the sound of its gentle flow soothes your soul. You dip your fingers into the cool water and feel a sense of refreshment wash over you, as if any tiredness from the day is melting away.

Following the path further, you encounter a family of friendly butterflies. They dance around you, their wings fluttering like delicate pieces of art. The butterflies invite you to join in their graceful dance, and you twirl and spin with them, feeling light and carefree. Twirling and spinning. Spinning and twirling.

Next, you stumble upon a magical pond filled with shimmering koi fish. Each fish glides through the water, leaving a trail of rainbow colors behind them. You sit by the pond, watching the koi gracefully swim to and fro, feeling a sense of peace and harmony in their presence.

As you continue exploring the magical garden, you come across a grove of whispering trees. These trees have a special gift – they can communicate with one another through soft, musical rustles of their leaves. You sit beneath one of the trees, feeling embraced by their gentle whispers, and smiling knowingly as they share their ancient wisdom with you.

The garden is not only home to plants and animals but also to tiny fairies that flit about like iridescent fireflies. They playfully tease you, their laughter sounding like the tiniest jingling bells. The fairies invite you to join in their games, and you play hide-and-seek among the flowers, feeling the magic of the garden coursing through your veins as you dart behind the plants and jump out, surprising the little fairies. Darting and jumping. Jumping and darting.

As the night progresses, you find yourself in a meadow of glowing mushrooms. The mushrooms emit a soft, radiant light that illuminates the darkness around you. It's as if you're surrounded by a galaxy of tiny stars, and you lie down in the soft grass, feeling the gentle hum of the earth beneath you.

In the heart of the magical garden, there stands a grand, ancient tree, its branches stretching towards the heavens. This tree is the Tree of Dreams, and it's said to grant peaceful slumber and the sweetest dreams imaginable to all who seek its shelter. You lean against the tree's sturdy trunk, feeling its comforting presence enveloping you.

Under the Tree of Dreams, you close your eyes and listen to the sounds of the night. The soft chirping of crickets and the distant hoot of an owl lull you into a state of deep relaxation. The magic of the garden wraps around you like a warm blanket, and you feel a sense of oneness with the world around you.

Mindful Magic

As the night deepens, the stars above seem to shine even brighter, guiding you to a realm of dreams. The dreams dance around you, teasing and tempting you as you're guided gently into your cozy bed. You begin to feel the weight of your body pulling you down like a magnet, drawing you down into your cushiony bed.

You surrender to the tranquility of the magical garden, allowing the magic to carry you into a peaceful, dreamy slumber. Your mind drifts off to a world of imagination and wonder, where you can fly with the fairies, swim with the fish, and dance with the butterflies.

Sleep tight, dear child, for the magical garden will always be here to welcome you on your next enchanting journey. May your dreams be filled with joy and adventure. Goodnight.

Guided Meditation: Island of Dreams

Once upon a starlit night, as the moon casts a silvery glow over the world, you find yourself nestled cozily in your bed, ready for a magical adventure. Take a deep breath, close your eyes, and imagine yourself sitting on a dock by the edge of the ocean. The blue sky above is clear, except for a few fluffy white clouds that float overhead.

Off in the distance, you notice a small sailboat making its way toward you. It approaches closer and closer to you until it is right in front of you. The sails flutter and wave in the gentle breeze, inviting you to climb aboard.

You step onto the boat and feel a wave of love wash over you. You immediately feel safe and know that you are protected wherever you go. The boat sets sail once more and you begin your journey, sailing off across the vast ocean.

The sound of gentle waves lapping against the boat's hull lulls you into a state of calm and relaxation. As the boat sails on, you see an island on the horizon. It's a deserted tropical paradise, surrounded by turquoise waters and swaying palm trees. The island beckons you with its promise of adventure and tranquility.

Mindful Magic

As your boat glides onto the sandy shore, you step onto the warm, golden sand. The island welcomes you with a soft breeze that carries the scent of blooming flowers and the salt of the sea. You feel the sand beneath your toes, grounding you in the moment.

The island is a treasure trove of wonders waiting to be discovered. You wander along a winding path, bordered by lush tropical plants. The leaves are vibrant shades of green, and some are so large they could be umbrellas. You feel like a tiny explorer in a magical land.

Following the path, you come across a hidden waterfall. The water cascades down into a crystal-clear pool, inviting you to take a refreshing dip. You wade into the water, feeling its cool embrace, washing away any worries or cares that might have lingered in your mind.

The waterfall's gentle melody becomes a calming tune, putting your mind at ease. The water cascades down splashing into the pool below. Cascading and splashing. Splashing and cascading.

As you continue your journey, you encounter a family of playful monkeys swinging from the trees. They chatter and giggle, beckoning you to join in their joyful play. You climb up, up, up into the trees, feeling the excitement of adventure coursing through your body.

The monkeys teach you to swing gracefully from branch to branch, and you feel like a true jungle explorer. Swinging and leaping. Leaping and swinging.

Next, you stumble upon a hidden cove with shallow, turquoise waters teeming with colorful fish. The fish seem to dance in the sunlight, their scales gleaming like precious gems. You dip your fingers into the water, and the fish tickle your skin as they playfully swim around you. It's as if they're welcoming you to their underwater kingdom.

Further along, you discover a secret garden filled with exotic flowers in every hue imaginable. The flowers emit a sweet, enchanting fragrance that fills the air. You lie down among the flowers, feeling the soft petals beneath you, and gaze up at the clear blue sky. Gazing up at the sky, you can spot shapes in the fluffy clouds above.

As the day turns to dusk, you find yourself on a serene stretch of beach, where the sand feels like velvet beneath your feet. The setting sun paints the sky in shades of pink and orange, creating a breathtaking canvas overhead. You sit on the sand, watching the sun dip below the horizon, and feel a sense of peace wash over you.

As the stars start to twinkle in the night sky, you build a small bonfire on the beach. The crackling flames create a warm glow, and you sit by the fire, feeling its comforting heat. Friendly island creatures emerge from the plants to join you around the fire, basking in its warmth. You toast marshmallows and tell stories, feeling the bonds of friendship and love with the island and its inhabitants.

With the night deepening, you lay down on a soft blanket, gazing up at the stars. Each star seems to hold a secret, and you imagine all the dreams and wishes that have been whispered to them over the ages. You can feel your body becoming heavy and your eyes roll back as you find yourself guided gently back to your cozy bed. You snuggle into the covers and allow the island's magic to weave around you, cradling you in its embrace.

As the island drifts into slumber, you find yourself drifting off to a peaceful, dreamy sleep. You feel grateful for the enchanting adventure you've had on the deserted tropical island, and you know that it will always be a place of comfort and serenity in your heart. Sleep tight, dear child, and may your dreams be filled with the wonders of the island and the magic of the sea. Goodnight.

Guided Meditation: The Lullaby Express

Once upon a starry night, as the moon casts a gentle glow over the world, you find yourself snuggled warmly in your bed, ready for a magical journey. Take a deep breath, close your eyes, and imagine yourself standing on a platform at the Dreamland Station. The air is filled with the soothing melody of lullabies, and you feel a sense of anticipation and excitement in your heart.

Tonight is special, for you are about to embark on a magical journey aboard the Lullaby Express—a whimsical train that carries you to the realm of dreamland. As the clock strikes bedtime, a soft melody fills the air. It's the sweet sound of the Lullaby Express approaching, its gentle chugga-chugga-chugga-chugga echoing like a soothing lullaby. You can almost feel the gentle vibrations beneath you as the train comes to a stop right beside your bed.

The train's doors swing open with a whisper, inviting you to step aboard. As you cross the threshold, you're greeted by the train's warm, inviting interior. The seats are plush and comfy, and the walls are adorned with soft, pastel colors that seem to sway gently like a dance.

You find the perfect seat by the window and settle in, feeling the soft cushion embrace you. The train's conductor welcomes you with a knowing smile. "Welcome aboard the Lullaby Express, dear child," he says softly. "We're here to take you on a soothing journey to the land of dreams."

With a gentle push, the Lullaby Express begins to glide forward, and you're filled with a sense of serene excitement. As the train picks up speed, you watch as the world outside your window transforms. You're no longer in your room but surrounded by a dreamscape of wonder as the train chugs on. Chugga-chugga-chugga-chugga.

The train passes through fields of fluffy clouds, each one offering a glimpse into a different dream. You see castles made of cotton candy and rivers flowing with chocolate. You spot playful animals that wink and giggle as the train goes by, inviting you to join in their joyful frolic.

The conductor begins to hum a soothing tune, and you find yourself swaying in time with the melody. The gentle rhythm of the train's movement and the comforting melody combine, lulling you into a state of perfect relaxation. Your eyes grow heavy, and you let yourself drift into a dreamy trance. Chugga-chugga-chugga-chugga.

As the Lullaby Express continues its journey, you travel through a starlit sky, each star twinkling like a precious gem. You reach out and catch a handful of stardust, feeling its soft glow warm your palm. With a smile, you release the stardust into the air, watching as it sparkles and dances around you.

The train passes through fields of fluffy clouds, each one offering a glimpse into a different dream. You see castles made of cotton candy and rivers flowing with chocolate. You spot playful animals that wink and giggle as the train goes by, inviting you to join in their joyful frolic.

The conductor leans in closer, his wise eyes locking onto yours. "Dear child," he says, his voice a gentle breeze, "this is the land where dreams are born. With every breath you take, you embrace the tranquility of this realm, allowing your worries to melt away."

You nod in understanding, feeling a profound connection to the world around you. The train's journey is more than just a ride; it's a voyage of inner discovery, a pathway to the depths of your own peaceful being. Chugga-chugga-chugga-chugga.

As the Lullaby Express slowly comes to a stop, you realize you've arrived at your destination—the heart of dreamland. The conductor smiles at you and says, "This is where you'll have the sweetest dreams, my dear friend." The train's doors open once again, and you step out onto a landscape that shimmers with the colors of imagination.

In dreamland, you're met by a group of friendly animals who welcome you with open arms. Together, you embark on an adventure filled with laughter, exploration, and a sense of boundless joy as you leap and fly among rainbows with your new animal friends. With each step you take, your worries become lighter, and your heart feels freer.

The world of dreams welcomes you with open arms, and you feel an overwhelming sense of peace and happiness. As the night gently unfolds, the Lullaby Express begins its return journey to take you back home. You climb aboard once more, carrying with you the tranquility and wonder of dreamland.

The train's soothing melody plays softly in the background, wrapping you in a cocoon of calm. Chugga-chugga-chugga-chugga. With a contented sigh, you settle back into your seat, feeling the train's gentle movement carry you back to your room. Chugga-chugga-chugga-chugga.

As the Lullaby Express slows to a stop, you realize that the journey was not just a dream—it was a gift, a reminder that within you lies a world of serenity and magic.

You are guided gently back to your cozy bed, feeling the softness of your blankets and the warmth of your room. Your body begins to feel so heavy, you could sink right through your bed. The memory of the Lullaby Express lingers like a sweet lullaby in your heart.

As you drift into slumber, you carry with you the peacefulness of the journey, knowing that whenever you close your eyes, the Lullaby Express is ready to carry you to the land of dreams once more.

Sleep peacefully, dear child, and let the magic of the Lullaby Express guide you into a night filled with dreams as enchanting as the stars in the sky. Goodnight.

Guided Meditation: Unicorn Dreamland

Once upon a magical evening, in a world where dreams hold extraordinary power, you find yourself snuggled up in your bed. As the moon casts its soft, silvery glow through your window, you nestle under your cozy blankets, ready to begin your nightly adventure. Closing your eyes, you take a deep, calming breath.

In your mind's eye, a swirling mist of pastel colors appears, gradually shaping into a magical portal. This portal is your gateway to the world of Unicorn Dreamland. As you step through the portal, a wave of love washes over you and you instantly know you are safe and protected wherever you go.

You find yourself in a breathtaking meadow filled with vibrant flowers and shimmering butterflies. The air is sweet, carrying the soothing scent of lavender. Glistening streams meander through the meadow, their gentle babbling harmonizing with the soft breeze rustling the leaves of ancient trees.

In the distance, you spot a group of playful unicorns with coats as white as snow and manes that flow like ribbons of silk. Their eyes sparkle with kindness, and their laughter sounds like tinkling chimes. One unicorn, named Stardust, approaches you with a gentle nudge.

"Welcome, dear child," Stardust greets. Her voice is like a melodious lullaby. "We've been waiting for you. Are you ready for a wondrous adventure?"

With a heart full of excitement, you nod, and Stardust lowers her graceful head. You climb onto her back, feeling the warmth of Stardust's presence wrap around you like a comforting embrace. With a graceful leap, you are off, soaring over meadows and forests, your journey guided by the silver glow of the moon.

Together, you fly through a sky painted with hues of pink and purple, passing by stars that wink and twinkle, whispering secrets of dreams. Below, a cascading waterfall creates a soothing melody, and as you glide through its mist, a sense of pure tranquility washes over you.

Stardust leads you to the heart of Unicorn Dreamland—a serene, magical garden. In this garden, flowers sing soft melodies, their petals opening and closing in harmony. You reach out and touch a petal, feeling a wave of calmness flow through your fingertips.

"Here, dear child, you can plant your own dreams," Stardust says, guiding you to a patch of soft, glowing earth. With closed eyes, you imagine your happiest thoughts, your dreams taking the form of shimmering seeds. With a gentle touch, you plant them in the ground, knowing they will blossom into beautiful moments of joy.

Continuing your journey, you approach a crystal-clear lake, its surface like a mirror reflecting the starry sky above. Landing by the water's edge, you see your own reflection shimmering back at you.

"Every ripple on this lake holds a wish," Stardust whispers. You close your eyes and make a wish, sending it into the water with a gentle toss of a pebble. A sense of hope and positivity fills your heart as if your wish is already being carried away by the universe.

As the night gently wanes, Stardust guides you back to the meadow where your journey began. With a tender smile, Stardust nuzzles you, her eyes filled with kindness and wisdom. "It's time for you to return, dear child," Stardust says softly. "Remember, Unicorn Dreamland is always here, waiting for you whenever you need its magic."

You embrace Stardust, feeling a deep sense of gratitude and love. Stepping back through the portal, the mist of colors envelops you as you return to your cozy bed. The portal closes behind you, leaving you in a state of tranquil bliss.

As you wrap yourself up in the warmth of your blankets, your body begins to feel heavy, as though you could sink right through your bed. You feel a serene slumber settle over you. The memories of your magical journey dance in your mind, carrying you into a peaceful and dreamy sleep.

As you drift off, Stardust's gentle presence lingers, whispering sweet dreams and wishes fulfilled. And so, dear child, as you close your eyes and embrace the night, remember that Unicorn Dreamland will always be there, waiting for you.

With a heart full of love and a mind full of dreams, you too can embark on your journey to a world where unicorns play and wishes come true. Sleep peacefully sweet child, and may your dreams be as enchanting as the stars that light up the night sky.

Conclusion

Embracing the Magic

As parents, we often find ourselves tirelessly searching for ways to ensure our children have peaceful and restful nights. The bedtime routine is crucial in setting the tone for a good night's sleep, and one powerful tool that we have at our disposal is bedtime meditations.

In this concluding chapter, we invite you to embrace the magic of bedtime meditations and unlock the full potential of these soothing and transformative experiences. Bedtime meditations offer a unique opportunity to create a calming atmosphere that allows children to unwind, let go of their worries, and drift into peaceful slumber.

Through the power of storytelling, visualization, and gentle guided imagery, children can tap into their imagination and create a tranquil space within the mind to embark on dreamy adventures that transport them to a world of relaxation and tranquility. By incorporating meditations into their bedtime routine, parents can create a calming experience that promotes relaxation and a sense of security.

The benefits of bedtime meditations extend beyond a good night's sleep. Regular practice can help children develop essential skills such as mindfulness, emotional regulation, and self-soothing techniques. By teaching your child to connect with their breath, embrace their imagination, and cultivate a sense of inner stillness, you empower them with valuable tools they can carry into their daily lives.

One of the key benefits of bedtime meditations is their ability to instill a sense of inner peace. Through imaginative journeys, children learn to let go of the day's worries and anxieties, allowing their minds to unwind and find solace. They are transported to magical dreamlands where they can feel safe, loved, and empowered.

A consistent bedtime routine that includes calming meditation stories helps soothe common childhood concerns such as fear of the dark, separation anxiety, and self-confidence issues so children can learn to overcome their fears and develop a sense of inner strength. Moreover, bedtime meditations provide an opportunity for parents and children to connect on a deep level.

By participating in these meditative journeys together, parents can create a bond of trust and understanding with their children. By engaging in these soothing rituals, you create a special and intimate connection with your child. This shared experience fosters open communication, empathy, and emotional resilience.

Your child will fall asleep feeling safe, loved, and empowered, ready to embrace the adventures that await them in their dreams. By introducing your child to these magical bedtime stories, you provide them with a safe space to explore their emotions and find inner peace. As they immerse themselves in the enchanting tales, their minds become calm, their bodies relax, and a sense of serenity washes over them.

Dreamy Bedtime Meditations for Children

So, dear parents, it's time to embark on this beautiful adventure of bedtime meditations. These meditations are a gateway to a world of relaxation, where worries melt away and dreams take flight. Embrace the magic on this journey towards peaceful nights and happier, well-rested days. Watch as your child drifts off into a world of peaceful slumber, free from worries and filled with dreams. Goodnight and sweet dreams to you and your little ones.

ABOUT THE AUTHOR

Kaela Green Carter is a dedicated parent, author, and child psychologist who is deeply committed to the well-being of children and all of humanity through her work and her writing. With a Master's degree in Counseling Psychology, along with certifications in education and hypnotherapy, Kaela brings over a decade of experience, aiming to empower children and adults with essential skills to enrich their lives.

Her passion for promoting mindfulness and emotional healing inspires her to guide others on their own healing journeys toward self-awareness, inner peace and oneness. Kaela's mission is to make the practice of mindfulness and meditation accessible and enjoyable to people of all ages, especially children, as they are our future. Through her beautifully crafted books, she seeks to equip children and their caregivers with invaluable tools to help them find peace within themselves, while navigating the challenges of growing up and living in our chaotic world.

Her experience, expertise, and enthusiasm for embracing and igniting young hearts and minds make Kaela's books a cherished resource for families, educators, and therapists alike. The foundation of emotional resilience and inner peace promoted through her books allows people of any age the freedom to blossom into their most authentic selves.

THE MINDFUL MAGIC SERIES

Let the magic of meditation nurture your child's mind, body, & soul. Empower them with mindfulness today to sow the seeds of serenity and inner peace for a happier tomorrow.

The tools in this empowering children's series help kids:

~**Calm their busy minds** into serene stillness
~**Embrace mindfulness** as a peaceful escape from everyday stress or pressure
~**Spark emotional growth** and navigate challenges with newfound courage
~**Manage negative thoughts** and find tranquility in the midst of big emotions
~**Unlock inner peace** by embracing awareness in the present moment
~**Transform restless nights** into soothing slumbers
~**Find inner calm** and improve their focus and concentration
~**Boost self-esteem** and realize their limitless potential

Within the titles of this transformative book series created by child psychologist and fellow parent, **Kaela Green Carter,** you'll uncover a treasure trove of mindful solutions designed specifically for your child's needs. **Through tranquil meditations, engaging exercises, and practical techniques, children are gently guided on a journey toward self-empowerment.**

Explore the magic within each book, and watch as **stress and anxiety melt away, positive thinking and self-esteem flourish, and anger transforms into understanding and connection**. With **'Mindful Magic,'** you hold the key to unlocking a magical world of inner peace and harmony, empowering your child to master their emotions and navigate life's challenges with grace and resilience.

Join a mindful community of parents who are dedicated to building awareness, confidence, happiness, and inner peace in their children. The children are the future. To view this series on Amazon click the QR code below. **Let's create a magical tomorrow by making our children mindful today.**

Dreamy Bedtime Meditations for Children

We hope you've enjoyed
Dreamy Bedtime Meditations for Children.
It's through your support and reviews that this book is able to reach the hands, minds, and hearts
of more parents and children.
Please kindly take a moment to leave a review on
Amazon. Please scan the QR code below.
If you reside in a country that isn't listed, please use the link provided in your Amazon order.

Please follow these simple steps to leave a review for this book:
1. Open the camera on your phone
2. Hover it over the QR code below
3. Leave a review once you're taken to the appropriate page

All it takes is a minute to make a difference.
Thank you for your support!

Bibliography

Cheng, K.S., et al. (2019). "Heart rate variability of various viseo-aided mindful deep breathing durations and its impact on depression, anxiety, and stress symptom severity." Mindfulness. https://doi-org.proxy1.ncu.edu/10.1007/s12671-019-01178-8

Crescentini, C., et al. (2016). "Mindfulness-Oriented Meditation for Primary School Children: Effects on Attention and Psychological Well-Being. Frontiers in Psychology," vol. 7. Retrieved from: https://doi.org/10.3389/fpsyg.2016.00805

Garey, J., et al. (2023). "The power of mindfulness: how a meditation practice can help kids become less anxious, more focused." Child Mind Institute. Retrieved from: https://childmind.org/article/the-power-of-mindfulness/

Lupino, F. (2023). "Health Disparities in Pediatric Sleep." Sleep Medicine Clinics, vol. 18, no. 2, (pp.225-234). Retrieved from: https://doi.org/10.1016/j.jsmc.2023.01.005

Mindell, J.A., et al. (2009). "Developmental aspects of sleep hygiene: Findings from the 2004 National Sleep Foundation Sleep in America Poll." Sleep Medicine, vol. 10, no. 7, (pp. 771-779). Retrieved from: https://doi.org/10.1016/j.sleep.2008.07.016

Mindell, J.A., et al. (2018). "Benefits of a bedtime routine in young children: sleep development and beyond. Sleep Medicine Reviews," vol. 57. https://doi.org/10.1016/j.smrv.2021.101425

Meltzer, LJ, et al. (2021). "Pediatric sleep health: it matters, and so does how we define it." Sleep Medicine Reviews, vol. 57. Retrieved from: https://doi.org/10.1016/j.smrv.2021.101425

Ordway, Monica R., et al. (2022). "Sleep deficiency in young children." Science Direct, vol. 43, no. 2, (pp. 229-237). Retrieved from: https://doi.org/10.1016/j.ccm.2022.02.007

Siversten, Borge, et. al. (2015). "Later Emotional and behavioral problems associated with sleep problems in toddlers: a longitudinal study." JAMA Pediatrics, vol. 169, no. 6, (pp. 575-582). Retrieved from: https://doi:10.1001/jamapediatrics.2015.0187

Turner, E.M. (2003). "The benefits of meditation: experimental findings." The Social Science Journal, vol. 40, no. 3, (pp. 465-470). Retrieved from: https://doi.org/10.1016/S0362-3319(03)00043-0

Connect with Kaela Green Carter

Dreamy Bedtime Meditations for Children is the first book in the Mindful Magic series. For more information please visit the series page using the QR Code below.

To discover more about Kaela Green Carter, please visit her website: https://kaelagreencarter.com/

View Kaela Green Carter's author page using the QR Code below.

Made in United States
Troutdale, OR
10/11/2023